"Charles Schulz is the only man we know who can make a round circle, a dash, a loop and two black spots express the following: an abiding love for Beethoven, a disillusionment with all women or an eight-day crusade of hate against a paper kite.

"If Charlie Schulz jiggles the circle, spots, dash and loop one way a comic strip character named Charlie Brown will tear your heart out with man's inhumanity to man. If he wiggles them a little differently he will set you to laughing so hard your sides will ache.

"The ability to make these little ink scratches into facial expressions is, of course, the mark of the great cartoonist—and Charlie Schulz has been voted the greatest of them all by the National Cartoonists Society."

—*New York World Telegram and Sun*

YOU'RE
A WINNER,

CHARLIE BROWN!

by *CHARLES M. SCHULZ*

Selected Cartoons from GO FLY A KITE, CHARLIE BROWN VOL. I

FAWCETT CREST • NEW YORK

A Fawcett Crest Book
Published by Ballantine Books
Copyright © 1959, 1960 by United Feature Syndicate, Inc.

ISBN 0-449-21458-3

This book comprises the first half of GO FLY A KITE, CHAR-LIE BROWN, and is published by arrangement with Holt, Rine-hart & Winston, Inc.

Printed in Canada

First Fawcett Crest Edition: November 1966
First Ballantine Books Edition: November 1987

WHEN I GET BIG, I'M GOING TO BE A HUMBLE LITTLE COUNTRY DOCTOR

I'LL LIVE IN THE CITY SEE, AND EVERY MORNING I'LL GET UP, CLIMB INTO MY SPORTS CAR AND ZOOM INTO THE COUNTRY!

THEN I'LL START HEALING PEOPLE...I'LL HEAL EVERYBODY FOR MILES AROUND!

I'LL BE A WORLD FAMOUS HUMBLE LITTLE COUNTRY DOCTOR!

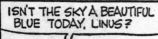

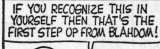

SO CHARLIE BROWN HAD A BABY SISTER LAST NIGHT!

BOY, THERE SURE WAS A LOT OF EXCITEMENT AROUND HERE ABOUT MIDNIGHT...PEOPLE RUNNING IN ALL DIRECTIONS...

..CARS COMING AND GOING.. TELEPHONES RINGING...THINGS STILL HAVEN'T CALMED DOWN.

AND IN ALL THE EXCITEMENT, NOBODY HAS REMEMBERED TO FEED THE DOG!

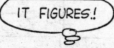

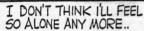

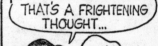

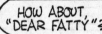

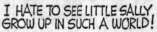